D1549037

Nancy Greene

Terry Barber

SPORTS
SERIES

Nancy Greene is published by
Grass Roots Press, a division of Literacy Services of Canada Ltd.

PHONE 1–888–303–3213
WEBSITE www.literacyservices.com

ACKNOWLEDGEMENTS

We acknowledge the financial support of the Government of Canada through the Book Publishing Industry Development Program (BPIDP) for our publishing activities.

We acknowledge the support of
the Alberta Foundation for the Arts
for our publishing programs.

Editor: Dr. Pat Campbell
Image research: Dr. Pat Campbell
Book design: Lara Minja, Lime Design Inc.

Library and Archives Canada Cataloguing in Publication

Barber, Terry, date
        Nancy Greene / Terry Barber.

ISBN 978-1-894593-60-1

        1. Greene, Nancy, 1943– . 2. Skiers—Canada—Biography.
3. Readers for new literates. I. Title.

PE1126.N43B3635 2007   428.6'2   C2007-902780-6

Printed in Canada.

Contents

An Esso ad, 1964.

Tiger

It is the 1960s. An oil company runs ads in Canada. The ads are about Esso. If you buy gas at Esso, you will get a **bonus**. You will "put a tiger in your tank." Your car will run better.

The Canadian ski team.
(Nancy is in the middle row, third from the left.)

Tiger

In 1965, Nancy Greene is a star skier.
Nancy is on the Canadian ski team.
The skiers have nicknames. An artist
paints the nicknames on their helmets.

Nancy
is on the
Canadian ski team
from 1959
to 1968.

Nancy wears her "Tiger" helmet.

Tiger

Nancy does not have a nickname. Nancy thinks of the Esso ads. She likes the "Put a tiger in your tank" ads. Nancy gives herself a nickname. She calls herself "Tiger." The artist paints "Tiger" on Nancy's ski helmet.

Nancy races down the hill.

Tiger

Tiger is the perfect nickname. Nancy is like a tiger on the ski hill. She is fast and has no fear. She has great talent. She also works hard. Nancy will become Canada's best skier ever.

Nancy Greene, age 3 months.

Early Years

Nancy Greene is born in Ottawa in 1943. She is born during World War II. Her parents are from British Columbia. After the war, the Greenes move back to British Columbia. They move to Rossland.

World War II goes from 1939 to 1945.

Rossland is in the Kootenay Mountains.

Rossland, British Columbia.

14

Early Years

Rossland is ski country. It is in the heart of the mountains. It gets lots of snow. In 1897, Rossland hosted the first ski races in Canada. If you love to ski, Rossland is a great place to live.

Nancy stands with her brothers and sisters.
(Nancy is second from the left.)

Early Years

The Greene family loves to ski. Nancy has two sisters and three brothers. All of them learn to ski. They are all on skis by the age of three. Nancy loves the sport. She is also very good at it.

Nancy learns to ski on wooden skis.

Nancy skis in a high school race.

The Will to Win

By the late 1950s, Nancy is ski racing.
She loves to compete. In 1958, Nancy
wins her first **trophy**. She wins a
trophy for coming in second place.
Nancy's older sister gets first place.

The 1960 Olympics are held in Squaw Valley, California.

The Olympic ski team, 1960.

The Will to Win

In 1960, Nancy and her older sister compete in the Olympics. Nancy and her sister do not win medals. Nancy learns from these Olympics. She knows she wants to win a gold medal.

Nancy and her older sister, 1960.

Nancy runs to get strong.

The Will to Win

Nancy works and trains hard. She goes to school in the fall and spring. In the winter, she skis. During the summer, she works hard to get strong. Nancy lifts weights. Nancy is one of the first women skiers to lift weights.

An Olympic gold medal from 1968.

The Will to Win

School. Skiing. Training. Nancy does not have a "normal" student life. Nancy never feels she is missing out. Nancy knows where she is headed. She is headed toward Olympic gold.

The Innsbruck Olympics, 1964.

The Will to Win

It is 1964. It is an Olympic year. Nancy does not win her gold medal. She has the **will** to win. Nancy likes to "go like hell" when she skis. Nancy needs more than the will to win. She needs to fine-tune her skiing.

The winter Olympics are held every four years. The 1964 Olympics are in Innsbruck, Austria.

Nancy Greene holds the World Cup.

The Olympic Gold

Nancy is the first skier to win the World Cup title.

Nancy keeps up her hard work. Her skills grow with each year. She wins the first ever World Cup in 1967. Nancy is the best woman racer in the world. Can she win a gold medal in the 1968 Olympics?

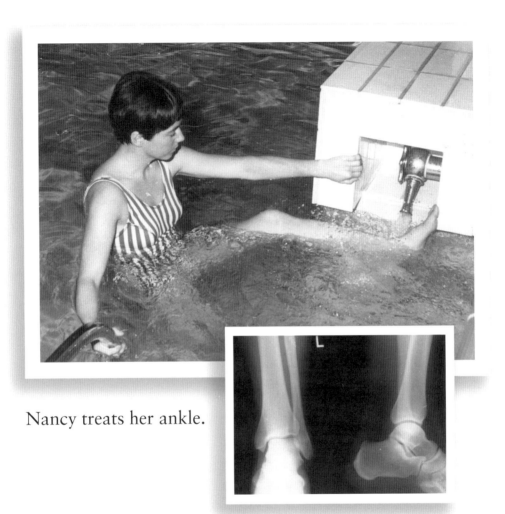

Nancy treats her ankle.

An x-ray of Nancy's ankle.

The Olympic Gold

The 1968 Olympics do not look good
for Nancy. She has hurt her ankle.
Her training suffers. Her belief in
herself suffers. Nancy knows she must
be positive. Nancy must believe she
can win.

The
1968 winter
Olympics are held in
Grenoble, France.

Nancy comes in 10th place.

The Olympic Gold

Nancy has three chances to win a gold medal. In her first race, she comes in 10th place. Nancy is sad. She feels sorry for herself. She knows she can do better. Nancy needs to calm her mind. She needs to "go like hell."

Nancy goes like hell.

Nancy comes in second place.

The Olympic Gold

In her second race, Nancy goes for it.
She skis well. She wins a silver medal.
Many skiers would be happy with
a silver medal. Nancy is not. Nancy
knows she can do even better. Nancy
wants the gold medal.

Nancy wins the gold medal.

The Olympic Gold

"Perfect." Perfect is how Nancy skis in her third race. She attacks the hill with all she has. It is as if her skis have wings. Nancy wins her gold medal. Nancy calls this race her best ever. Canada cheers her win.

Nancy wins her gold medal by 2.64 seconds. Most skiers win races by a **millisecond**.

Nancy retires from ski racing.

After the Olympics

Nancy Greene retires from ski racing in 1968. She is 24 years old. She has won her Olympic gold medal. She has won two World Cups. As a skier, Nancy has reached her goals.

Nancy wins her second World Cup in 1968.

Nancy and her husband, Al Raine, 1969.

After the Olympics

Nancy uses her great energy to achieve
other goals. She marries Al Raine in
1969. Their twin sons are born the
next year. She and her husband help
develop ski **resorts**.

Willy
competes
in the 1984
Olympics.

Nancy and her sons, Willy and Charley.

Nancy inspires children.

After the Olympics

Nancy promotes skiing for children.
She **inspires** children to become skiers.
Nancy is a hero to them. Some of the
children follow Nancy's footsteps.
They ski for Canada.

Nancy holds her Olympic medals, 1999.

Athlete of the Century

After Nancy retires from skiing, she gets many awards. In 1999 Nancy gets an award that sets her apart. Nancy is named Canada's Female Athlete of the 20th Century. Canada honours the skiing "Tiger" as the best of the best.

Nancy gets the Order of Canada in 1968.

Glossary

bonus: an extra benefit.

inspire: to encourage somebody to do something.

millisecond: one-thousandth (.001) of a second.

resort: a place where people go for pleasure or sport.

trophy: an award for success. The trophy is usually a silver or gold cup.

will: a firm wish or desire.

Talking About the Book

What did you learn about Nancy Greene?

What words would you use to describe Nancy?

Do you think "Tiger" is a good nickname for Nancy? Why or why not?

What did Nancy do to reach her goals?

The author says that Nancy has "the will to win." What does this mean?

Picture Credits